LIFE AFTER
THE STORM

Debbie Fleitman

Library of Congress Control Number: 2014913012

ISBN-10: 0692260188
ISBN-13: 978-0692260180

To Danny, Tara, Rylee, and Nyla

You gain strength, courage and confidence by every experience in which you really stop to look fear in the face....You must do the thing which you think you cannot do.

~ Eleanor Roosevelt

TABLE OF CONTENTS

Preface 1

Introduction 3

Joplin, Missouri 5

Family 7

Sunday, May 22, 2011 11

Path of Destruction 32

Healing and Recovery 35

Finding a New Home 42

Jack 48

A Second Chance 51

Developments 54

Three Years Later 56

Afterward 58

Acknowledgments 62

Preface

In my many years of writing as a student, teacher, and author of short published articles, I never envisioned writing a non-fiction book about tornado victims. My novel was to be about memorable characters whose abundant conflicts were solved by the end of the book. With Harper Lee as my muse, I planned to write the great American novel. But....

Throughout my life's journeys, opportunities have surfaced in unique ways. My oldest daughter, April, moved to Springfield, Missouri, with her husband in 2006, and they became friends with Tara and Danny Graves. Slowly the Graves' story unfolded, and April convinced me that their journey as survivors of the Joplin tornado needed to be written.

I began writing this book in June 2012, thirteen months after the tornado. After numerous interviews with the family, I, too, agreed their moving story must be shared with others. I hope the message that is conveyed in this book will inspire readers and help them remember that during their darkest hours, there is always hope.

Through my research I found a large amount of conflicting data on many facts and statistics. I chose to document one source and listed the information as thus. All words in quotations in this book are direct quotes by the people who were there.

Chapter 1

Introduction

As morning dawned in Joplin, Missouri, on May 22, 2011, it was a normal day in the community of over 50,000. The pulse and the rhythm of the city were like that of any Sunday in spring. It was overcast with a cool waft of air that characterized the climate of the Ozark area. Families ate their breakfast as they readied for church services; others prepared for a normal day at work. Doctors and nurses arrived at the local hospitals to care for their patients, while workers at restaurants and retail establishments prepared to service all their patrons. Joplin High School seniors were especially excited about the day they had been anticipating for twelve years – graduation. They looked forward to the highly awaited, fun-filled day of congratulations, hugs, diplomas, and graduation parties. The afternoon became a perfect, sunny Sunday that allowed families to rest and enjoy each other's company. It was just another normal Sunday in Joplin, Missouri.

Normalcy - a typical day for so many would end in disaster and death as the deadliest tornado in six decades, an EF-5, roared for twenty minutes to annihilate one-third of the town of Joplin.

The monstrous tornado that day in Joplin had little mercy on its residents or structures. It violently ripped through the core of the city and continued in a southwest direction, leaving a deadly mark of carnage and unbelievable destruction along its path. Through every disaster, natural or not, stories emerge of people who experience the worst, yet through their resilient spirits, they not only survive but thrive. Their harrowing experience makes their daily walk through life a calculated appreciation that every minute is a cherished gift.

This book is about such a family. Danny, Tara, Rylee, and Nyla Graves survived the most devastating tornado in seven years in the United States when all odds and forces of nature were against them. Their survival is a testament that a higher authority allowed them to continue to have life and be thankful for every breath they take.

Chapter 2

Joplin, Missouri

Joplin, Missouri, (50,150) lies in Southern Jasper County and Northern Newton County in the Southwest corner of Missouri. It is the largest city in Jasper County but is not the county seat. The city was founded in 1873 as a zinc mining community. Manufacturing is the largest industry there, and the median age of the residents is thirty-five. The historic Route 66 runs through the town that has six colleges, including Missouri Southern State University. It is also home to Joplin Regional Airport, and it is the birthplace of author Langston Hughes.

Typically, Missouri is not a state listed in Tornado Alley. There is much debate and differing opinions on exactly which states belong in the area because of the criteria and data used. Statistics show that 95% of all tornados are below an EF-3 intensity, and only a few (0.1% of all tornados) achieve an EF-5 status. From 1991-2010, the United States had a yearly average of 1253 tornados. Missouri had forty-five compared to Texas with 155 tornados; therefore, the tornado that hit Joplin was an anomaly that defied the statistics.

Historically, tornado activity in Joplin is above the Missouri state average. There is a 199% greater chance of having a tornado in Joplin than the U.S. average in other cities. The Joplin area is no stranger to violent weather. On April 3, 1956, an EF-4 tornado touched down and injured fifty-nine people. Another EF-4 tornado occurred on May 10, 2008, killing fifteen and injuring 200 people. The May 22, 2011, tornado in Joplin would surpass the previous statistics and forever leave an imprint of its violent destruction on its residents.

Chapter 3

Family

In May 2011 the Graves were a normal middleclass family with two little girls Rylee, 5 and Nyla, 3 - who were the pride and joy of the family. Tara Sanders Graves, 29 and Danny Graves, 28 both were Joplin natives and had been together for seven years. They and their daughters lived in the house that Danny's great-grandparents, Tom and Virginia Frossard, had built in 1973. The Frossards literally built the house on their own with help from only family and friends. It was a ranch-style home with 1600 square feet, three bedrooms, two baths, and a two-car garage. It was an exceptionally open floor plan for its time.

At the time of Tom and Virginia's deaths, the house was left to their daughter Carol, and when she passed, the house was given to Danny's mother Shelley Graves. At the estate sale, Shelley confided in her son that she really did not want to sell the home because it had been in the family for so many years, but financially she could not afford to maintain or renovate it. Danny and Tara decided to take the weathered house, remodel it, and make it their home. The renovation took over a year, and after a much-extended budget, in 2005 the Graves finally called 1826 Connecticut Avenue their home.

As with many parents, Tara and Danny centered their whole world on their daughters. Both are beautiful young ladies who enjoy life to its fullest. Rylee is a sweet, "little old soul" who is precocious in nature and is constantly in deep discussions with her parents. She has wisdom beyond her years. Her thin blond hair frames her pear-shaped face, and her sky-blue eyes are always filled with wonderment. As a small child she always had a motherly instinct, always taking care of her little sister; she is a sensitive, kindhearted child who truly cares about others. She always says that she wants to be a "people doctor" or an "animal doctor." She is the quintessential "All-American girl" who loves to sing and dance and is always ready for a new experience. She woke up on May 22, 2011, a normal little girl, but by nightfall, she would have experienced an event that would change her for life.

Another little girl was added to the family when Rylee was eighteen months old, and she was named Nyla. She completed the family in an amazing way. It was challenging for the Graves raising two little girls while they were working, paying bills, and going through life's everyday struggles. She too has thin, straight hair, and looks more like her father than Rylee. Nyla is the family comedienne. Although she appears to be shy around those who do not know her, she finds humor and laughter in the most ordinary places. Nyla always appears to be thinking of the next punch line and indulges in pleasing others with

Rylee and Nyla visit a petting zoo three days before the tornado.

laughter. She is clever, and after a few minutes visiting with her, you soon forget she is just a young child. She too would be one of the unfortunate players in a drama that will unfold on the evening of May 22. Because she was so young - which was her salvation - she does not remember the horrific ordeal as much as her older sister.

Both girls share a bond that is indescribable. They complete each other as if they are twins. When one is weak, the other is strong, and they are truly best friends. This inseparable connection in body and soul was the impetus that was an integral part in their fight for survival and recovery.

Of course, every young family has a favorite pet, and the Graves family is no exception. Their loving, furry friend is Jack, a half-lab, half-German shepherd who is truly a mixture with the face and eyes of a lab and his color and coat a German shepherd. Jack was only four months old when the family bought him off *Craigslist* for only $50.00. A bed, kennel, and food came with the puppy, and it was a bonus that he was already house-trained. He had not been properly vaccinated; therefore, he contracted Parvo, which almost took his life. Tara and Danny claim that Jack is the best-behaved of dogs. He loves to swim, hunt, and play with Rylee and Nyla. He is truly a member of the family.

Chapter 4

Sunday, May 22, 2011

For the Graves family, May 22, 2011, started out as a typical day. The family hurried through their breakfast of cereal, toast and juice and then attended services at Forest Park Baptist Church. They returned home, ate a quick sandwich, and Tara and the girls went to Dillon's, a local grocery store, for an afternoon of shopping and couponing. Tara was excited about being off work and taking it easy for the next two days. After the groceries were unloaded, she made a call to her older children from a previous marriage, Carsen, 10, and Olivia, 8, who live in Florida. The children were not home, and usually she did not leave a message, but that day she did. She simply said, "Love you; call me back."

1:40 P.M. *- Extremely strong air mass. Tornado watch is in effect with extremely strong super cells blowing over the next couple of hours. The main threat is large hail and strong tornadoes.*

That Sunday in May was a nice day, not too hot, and many were enjoying the springlike temperature. Turbulent storms were the norm during the early months of spring, and the Graves were aware that the weather could become severe. As in all marriages spousal arguments occur, and Tara and Danny's relationship was no different. They had an argument that morning that was so trivial that later they could not remember why they had bickered. Tara felt she needed some time to cool off, so she and the girls went for a drive. She knew there was a possibility of storms that night, and the weather conditions seemed abnormally still and quiet. She lost track of time while driving and soon realized that she needed to return home because she did not want to be caught in a storm. Life continued as normal with the girls finishing their homework and playing outside. Everyone was busy, but there were few words spoken between the couple. Danny was on his cell phone monitoring the weather while he was replacing parts on his meat smoker. Danny was passionate about cooking outdoors and planned to smoke a pork tenderloin for dinner that night -- a dinner that never transpired.

5:09 P.M. *- Tornado warning issued.*

Danny's hobby was to always check the weather conditions online. Joplin AS (Atmospheric Science) Weather was a site that Danny followed via Facebook. He considered this site to always be "spot on" with the weather conditions. The last prediction that was made by the blogger that day before signing off was, "I don't know what is going to happen; there is a build-up in Kansas, and it looks like the bad weather will be dumped on Joplin." Taking heed, Danny walked outside, and from his front porch he saw the wall cloud in Kansas, and the sky was light orange. He had seen these conditions many times before, so he was vigilant and continued checking the local weather.

5:11 P.M. - *Three minute siren alert sounded.*

Danny calmly entered his home and turned on KODE, the local television news channel. The tornado siren sounded for the first time; the weather was very still, with no rain or wind. As a precaution, the girls and Tara gathered pillows and blankets and climbed into the Jacuzzi bathtub in the master bathroom. Danny began his typical storm preparation. He turned off the attic fan, closed the windows, and watched the clouds from the living room window. He then saw the sky and got a sick feeling in his stomach. He had never had a feeling like this and tried to appear calm while inside he was an emotional rollercoaster. His heart was racing, and he felt he could not breathe. He tried to convince himself that what he saw in the sky would not become a reality.

5:34 P.M. - *Large hail started pelting Joplin, and a tornado formed west of the town.*

For the next few minutes nothing transpired, and like many little the girls, Rylee and Nyla were complaining that they were hot under the blankets. Thinking the threat was over and unaware of what lay ahead, Tara and the young girls left the bathtub, grabbed one of the girls' twin mattresses from their bunk bed, and walked a few steps to the hallway. The hallway led to the living room, so there was a clear view of the television. Tara and Danny were still not convinced that the weather conditions had improved, so

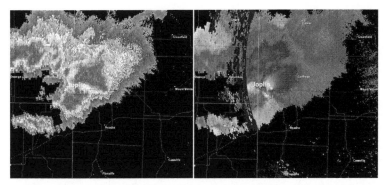

The radar on May 22, 2011, depicts the intensity of the tornado.

they continued watching the clouds and the news reports until the second siren sounded.

5:38 P.M. - Second three minute siren alert issued.

As the sirens blared, the weather anchor on KODE was screaming for all residents of Joplin to take cover, as the tornado footage encompassed the entire screen. The vibrant colors of yellow, red and the penetrating purple that colored the television screen showed the intensity of the deadly storm. When Tara and Danny saw the radar, their stomachs dropped; they knew it was too late to go to Dan's Grandma's basement. Paula Holland's home was just five minutes away, and they had usually gone there when bad weather prevailed. This was the only time the family did not; the rapidity and severity of the storm was upon them. They were captive in their own home. Tara began screaming as she looked at her daughters; she knew she could not protect them. She felt like a trapped mouse in a maze with no where to escape the impending doom. Every inch of her body was riddled with terror. Rylee looked at her mother, was alarmed, and asked if everything was okay, and Tara calmly reassured her that everything was fine. She was trying not to become hysterical, and she told her daughters she needed to "talk to Daddy and stay put—don't move!"

As the scene outside his home darkened, Danny stood at the front door trying to call his Grandma Holland, when his phone lost service. Tara knew by the look on Danny's face that the situation was dire, and then they were without electricity in total darkness. In seconds their world went from normalcy to insanity. They could see the pitch black sky, snapping power lines, and hear the vociferous roaring wind. Frantically, Danny screamed for Tara, Rylee, and Nyla to get in the hallway, and then the noise of the wind, rain, and spinning debris became deafening! It sounded like the earth was exploding – "like multiple bombs had gone off!" The tornado was so wide that they could not see it. The sky was just a wall of swirling ebony. The pounding rain hid the formation of multiple vortexes as the funnel touched down on Black Cat Road, five miles from the Graves' home. The Graves knew then they were helpless victims of the violent monster that would devour their home. They felt powerless and weak and knew they would not survive. Two thoughts crossed Tara's mind in the split seconds that followed: she wanted to tell Danny she was sorry about the argument, and she had not talked to Carsen or Olivia.

Danny ran to the hallway and screamed, "hold on to the girls—don't let them get away!" Tara, Rylee, and Nyla were face down in the hallway with their arms tucked underneath them. Danny threw the mattress on top of the girls and placed his arms around the mattress and held on for dear life. Their faithful companion, Jack, was by their side. Then the real nightmare began….

5:41 P.M. - *An EF-5 tornado touched ground on the southwest side of Joplin.*

The glass in the house began to explode; it sounded "rather melodic, in sync like music." The shards of shattered glass were circulating, hitting the walls and crashing into the television that was attached to the wall. The cylinder of spinning glass seemed to be a small tornado within their home. Danny described the sound as "a combination of a jet liner and freight train—It was Satan's vacuum." This seemed to last only seconds, and then there was an eerie moment of silence. Thinking that the worst had passed, Danny reassured his family that everything was going to be fine; he was in protection mode. The house then began to violently shake; the family "felt a yank, and then the roof was sucked off." It felt like they were "going down a rollercoaster and collapsing into the earth, being buried and turned inside out." It seemed like they were "thrown into space, and everything around them was caving in." Their home that they had loved and cherished became a demonic enemy and pounded their bodies with all the possessions that they once treasured. It was a slow motion nightmare that seemed to go on forever.

Nyla began screaming, but Rylee never uttered a whisper. Again, thoughts raced through Tara's mind. She prayed over and over again not for God to save her girls but instead not let them suffer. For the duration of the storm, they all kept their eyes closed, and the last thing Tara remembered was the splitting of the floor; "it felt like they were being thrown out of the house sideways." The sounds of breaking glass, splitting wood, and incomprehensible wind seemed to last forever. It seemed like hours, but in actuality it was about five minutes. Because the human mind and body are limited in their comprehension of such catastrophic events, Tara, Danny, and their little girls were not coherent during this unbelievable wrath of their home.

A Supreme Being had His watchful hand held over this family that evening.

5:49 P.M. - *The EF-5 tornado continued eastward.*

After the noise subsided, Danny awoke and shook Tara, and she opened her eyes for the first time. She felt disoriented like she had been sedated. Danny and Tara tried to sit up, but there was too much debris covering their bodies. Tara was on her back, and her first sight of the destruction around her brought disbelief. There were no trees, shreds of houses were everywhere, and Danny said, "It looked like hell on Earth or like a Stephen King movie." The rain and hail began coming down in torrents and felt like pellets hitting their bodies. She gasped and felt like she could not breathe or move. Pain enveloped every inch of her body. Danny had been hit on the back of his head by either a large piece of wood or a heavy metal object and felt like "it hit the life out of him." He had deep cuts on his

Minutes after the tornado the Graves' home lay in ruin.

head, legs, and arms. But he knew he had to pick himself up and help his family; "he could die later." Tara's injuries were more severe in nature than Danny's. Her right leg between the ankle and knee had been broken in two different places as if a toothpick had been snapped. She did not feel much pain because her "adrenaline had kicked in," and her whole body was numb. She felt "she could have lifted a car at that moment." The main focus of the couple was to find their little girls in the midst of the unbelievable destruction.

5:57 P.M. - *Tornado still on the ground and crossing I-44.*

A few minutes later, Tara and Danny heard Nyla screaming and knew she was near, but there was no sound from Rylee. Tara turned on her stomach, and in a frenzied motion she started throwing aside pieces of debris and other fragments in hope that Nyla would be under the wreckage of their home. Tara knew she had covered both girls with her body when they were in the hallway, so hopefully Nyla was under the pile of boards and splinters of wood. Tara continued to hear the screams which became louder the deeper she dug. Finally, she saw her youngest daughter's sweet face looking at her. Nyla's face was unrecognizable because it was plastered with dirt, twigs, mud, and blood, but she was the most beautiful sight to Tara. Overcome with hysterical emotion, Tara gently pulled her daughter from the rubble and knew that Nyla was not severely injured. The layers of boards, sheetrock, and splinters of wood were so deep that it actually acted as a cushion for the young girls' fragile bodies.

Danny and Tara continued to dig for Rylee and a few seconds later found her face up and eyes wide open. She was not crying, and there was such a "peace on her face." Tara immediately knew she was alive, but there was no

The family woke at this spot after the tornado.

expression on her face; she was in shock. Tara was euphoric and overcome with breathless sobs. Her body was trembling. Once again she had uncovered a daughter from the demise of their home. Both little girls had dirt and grime under their nails and in their noses and ears. Tears of joy erupted as the family of four held each other tenderly yet desperately. The family had not yet comprehended what had taken place; they were just happy to be alive. Then they saw hell....

As the Graves family had braced for the impact of the tornado, they had been held captive in its own funnel of destruction, spinning with unstoppable rotation. Their home had been picked up off its foundation, twisted and gyrated violently for about a hundred yards until it was annihilated. Their home had hit the barrier of three trees in their yard and exploded in air into a pile of unrecognizable rubble.

The trees were just a foot away from a transformer which possibly saved the home from catching fire.

In disbelief the Graves saw their whole neighborhood had been obliterated. They could see for miles because everything that was normally blocked by buildings or trees was flattened. Every possession, heirloom, or precious keepsake that had been an essential element in the patchwork of life that they called home was gone. A pink bicycle was wrapped around a tree like a piece of abstract art; and dolls, books, and framed pictures of loved ones were askew in the yards and street. Christmas decorations were hanging haphazardly in the trees and cars, and cinder blocks had been tossed about like Lego's. Tara's beloved piano was shattered and on its side amid the rubble. The Graves' cars had not moved, yet all the windows were broken, full of debris and wreckage with lumber and pieces

The front view of the family's home shows the destruction of the storm.

of metal on the roofs. The smell was unmistakable and overwhelming; it was like all liquids and solids in people's homes had been "put in a blender" and profusely heaved onto the terrain. Toys, furniture, doors, and cars looked like one mass of pulverized waste. All the buildings, houses, and apartment complexes on Connecticut Avenue between 15th and 26th Streets were completely destroyed.

Danny yelled to Tara that they had to get to the road and desperately hoped that someone would drive by and take them to the hospital. Danny's right foot was badly injured, and he was visibly impaired. Dark spots dotted his pupils, and everything he saw had a gray hue. He also had several lacerations on the right side of his head. He was trying to find a sense of peace in the madness of the moment and honestly did not know if his family was going survive but thought, "We are not going to die today." He found his cell phone, which was still working, but all cell towers were down. His immediate concern was Tara, Rylee, and Nyla; he knew he had to get them to the hospital. Until Tara tried to walk to the road, she had not realized her leg was just "hanging by threads." She knew she could not walk. At that point the hail was merciless, and the lightning was shockingly intense. Leaving Tara, Danny grabbed a piece of wood to cover the young girls and walked barefoot over the fifty feet of glass and miscellaneous debris until he could reach the road.

When Danny made it to the road, he yelled at the first car he saw, "Please stop and take my girls to the hospital!" The car did not stop. The next car was a 1990 Cavalier with a little elderly man, his wife, and grandson inside. Danny pleaded to the man to take his girls to the hospital, but the man insisted that he was not going to leave without all four of them. The monstrous hail, pouring rain, and sky-to-ground lightning were relentless, and it seemed to be

Remnants of the Graves' home illustrates the power of an EF-5.

freezing. The temperature had gone from warm to bitter cold within minutes. Danny helped the girls into the car but could not help Tara because he was so injured. The man, who was half the size of Tara, picked her up and carried her to his car; all four of the Graves family was crammed into the back seat.

Their savior started driving toward St. John's Medical Center, which was approximately a mile away; everyone gasped at the image of the building in view. St. John's had been severely damaged; curtains were flapping in the breeze where window panes had once been. Surveying the site seemed like a panoramic, slow motion movie. There were a sea of cars all toppled, crunched, and in a pile. The scene looked like a salvage yard. With urgency the man sped to Freeman Hospital which was just six blocks ahead, fearing that it too had been destroyed. It was a difficult journey to Freeman Hospital because the streets had been blocked by parts of houses, severed trees, and downed power lines. Rylee began to cry, so Tara started singing "Jesus Loves Me" to calm her and repeated the song until they reached the hospital. Tara and Danny's concern for the emotional as well as physical well-being of the girls was of the utmost importance. The girls were suddenly very quiet in the car, so Tara continually talked to them and made them talk. Finally, they arrived at Freeman Hospital.

6:16 P.M. - The tornado finally lifted east of Diamond, Missouri.

The Graves were lucky because they were some of the first victims to arrive that day. Doctors and nurses were running to the parking lot to help retrieve victims. The nurses were frantic yet collected as they opened the car door and took the little girls inside the hospital. Tara and Danny were finally relieved that their daughters were in good care. Next, the hospital staff took Tara and wheeled her in, and thus she was separated from the rest of the family. Tara was no longer in "mommy mode." At that point reality set in; she began screaming and was engulfed in pain.

The chaos in the hospital that night was unimaginable. Only four physicians were on duty in the ER that day, but it only took minutes for all hospital personnel who were employed at Freeman to arrive at the hospital to help the many victims. All 135 physicians came that day. Tara was put on a stretcher; a bottle of saline was poured over her severed leg and then wrapped. She was given a shot of morphine and was wheeled into the hallway on the first floor of the hospital and left alone.

Then the floodgates opened, with survivors arriving at an overwhelming rate. People with all types of injuries were brought in on two-by-fours and doors being used as stretchers. Every inch of the hospital lobby was filled with the injured -- some with life-threatening wounds and others with sustainable injuries. It was bedlam as the doctors, nurses, cleaning crew, and food staff tried to provide care to all and made split-second decisions to save those with near fatal injuries. Everyone was screaming for supplies and running down the halls. The hospital personnel divided the victims in the hallway: severe trauma on one side and non-life threatening injuries on the other. Because of lack of time and space, each victim's name was written on his/her arm with a black Sharpie. This was the hospital's only method of identification. Tara was scooted to the side, and every ten minutes random people would come by and give her another dose of morphine and quickly move on to the next patient.

As Tara lay there in pain, she was thinking of her girls. She knew they were in good hands because nurses took them as soon as they arrived. She was so thankful that their injuries were not severe. She wanted to know where they were but did not want to ask. Tara was awe-struck at witnessing atrocities that were equivalent to soldiers injured during war. Death was all around her. She saw victims with missing limbs and a person who was missing half of his face. Next to Tara, a man's knee cap was protruding about three or four inches while others were impaled by pieces of wood and poles. Like Tara, people's arms and legs were lifeless and hung from their bodies like a ragdoll. The worst were the sounds of those in the hallways. Some victims were moaning and crying for loved ones or screaming because of their debilitating pain. Although the smells experienced during the tornado were horrific, the sounds that she heard in the hospital are etched in her memory forever.

The hallway was so crowded that her knee was constantly bumped and knocked off the stretcher. Every inch of floor space was covered with victims, and hospital personnel were forced to step over the wounded as they administered aid. The hospital lobby looked like a tomb because it was operating on an emergency generator which left many areas dark and eerie. All medical personnel from throughout the city were flooding to the hospital. Freeman's staff had trained for a disaster but never envisioned that they would live and work through one. At that time the hospital did not know that St. John's Medical Center had been destroyed.

6:25 P.M. *- Hundreds of victims arrived at the hospital.*

When Danny finally arrived inside the hospital, he collapsed in a wheelchair. He was conscious but not consciously aware of the pain, and he could not see. Because his injuries were minor compared to others, he was

Vicki Cox and Rylee reunite at the one year anniversary of the tornado.

left unattended. He thought he was going to pass out and was alarmed because he had no vision. He constantly wondered where his daughters were, not knowing that they had been taken to the pediatric wing of the hospital.

As Danny waited, he could hear the cries and screams of desperation, and then a voice in the room asked, "Are you Danny Graves? I'm Aaron Garcia who went to school with you at Joplin High School." Danny was overjoyed to hear a familiar voice and told Aaron he needed something to drink. In the chaos Aaron found several bottles of water for Danny, and as he continued to drink them, his vision slowly recovered. He then saw the carnage that resulted from the tornado, an unimaginable sight to behold.

Because Danny's injuries were not life-threatening and space was needed at Freeman Hospital, he was moved to another hospital in Grove, Oklahoma, about thirty miles away. A paramedic in the ambulance had a cell phone and called Freeman to find information about Tara. She was told that Tara was in surgery. The paramedic also contacted Danny's mother and father; they were not injured and were ecstatic to hear from their son. At approximately at 8 P.M., he was finally given care. His injuries resulted in 200 staples in his left leg, twelve staples in his head, and skin grafts on his fingers that had six cuts to the bone.

Danny was in the hospital for a week and started making many phone calls and contacting insurance companies as soon as he was released. Although the family had nothing but the lives of those they loved, they were thankful for everything and every breath they took. After their tragedy, trivial things did not matter. There were no bad thoughts and no enemies. Danny's aunts and uncles, friends, and neighbors had also lost their homes. The Graves family had not one item to their name and nowhere to live, but the

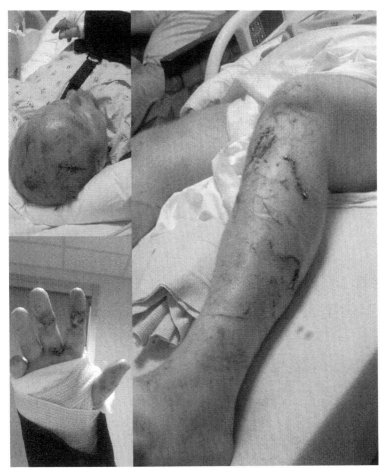

Danny's injuries from the tornado were severe.

remarkable kindness of others helped the family on their road to recovery. They knew the road would be long with many bumps and detours, but the future was their gift from God.

7:24 P.M. - The death toll was at 24.

Tara was eventually moved to the Cardiovascular Intensive Care Unit (CICU) upstairs. It was surreally quiet and still, a complete contrast to the chaos below. There were ten rooms with curtained partitions. Lying in the quiet room, Tara began thinking, "No one knows we are here." She tried to remember phone numbers but knew there was no phone service at the hospital. A nurse let Tara borrow her cell phone, so she called Danny's Grandma. Tara shouted, "We are all at Freeman alive!" Paula began crying hysterically when she received the call. After seeing the remains of the Graves' house, she was convinced that they had not survived. Next, she called her mother, and again there was disbelief that Tara and her family had escaped the wrath of the deadly tornado.

In urgency Dr. John Cox, a cardiovascular surgeon at Freeman, had arrived at the hospital. He surveyed the lobby that was wall-to-wall victims, saw more coming at an alarming speed, and immediately rushed home. He told his whole family -- wife Vickie, daughter Sarah and her fiancé Michael, sons Gabe and Aaron, and Aaron's fiancée McKenzie-- that they were all needed at the hospital immediately.

Sarah and Michael had just arrived at her parents' house. Sarah and Michael's home had been destroyed, and they had miraculously escaped injury in their cellar. They had walked over a mile through total chaos on their trek to her parents' house. They were coherent only by the overwhelming adrenaline that flooded their bodies. It was "fight or flight," so they continued through the deafening sounds of car and fire alarms, downed power lines, crushed cars, and people climbing out of the rubble that once was their homes. "It looked like a scene from *Lord of the Rings.*" Due to the ravage of the storm, there were no points of reference like street names and buildings; every landmark was gone or flattened. Sarah and Michael became disoriented and lost their direction many times before they arrived at her parents' home.

After hours of pain, reality started to kick in for Tara. The pain in her leg was unbearable, and she became distraught. No one had assessed Tara's leg in the CICU, yet the nurses continued to pour saline over her wounds and give her doses of morphine. A few minutes later still in excruciating pain, Tara heard a familiar voice; it was the voice of the father of Sarah Cox, Tara's good friend from high school. In desperation she cried out his name repeatedly, and when Dr. John Cox turned to look at Tara, he did not recognize her. She screamed, "I'm Tara Graves!" They embraced amid tears. He immediately took off her bandage and gasped at what he saw. The cuts and gashes on her leg were extensive; it was unrecognizable. She had broken her right femur; it was snapped in half with the bottom part dangling, and her tibia was also broken. She said that she did not know where her girls and Danny were and asked if Dr. Cox's wife, Vicki, could please find them. The Coxes lived in a home directly behind the hospital, and Tara knew Vicki would be there to help. Dr. Cox told her he would be right back and left to find an orthopedic surgeon he knew was at the hospital at that time.

As Dr. Cox was on his way to find a surgeon for Tara, his friend Dr. Derek Miller walked out of the elevator. Dr. Cox briefed him on Tara's wounds, and four hours after entering the hospital, Dr. Miller performed surgery. A metal rod was inserted in her leg where the tibia was broken, and several pins reattached the fibula. From the period of midnight to 5 A.M. that day, she has no memory. After surgery she awoke to excruciating pain. Many survivors had to wait for surgery, but because Tara had found Dr. Cox, she had surgery late that night. If he had not been there, she would have lost her leg. Many of those forced to wait had to have their limbs amputated.

When Sarah Cox arrived at the hospital, her father reported that Tara was in the cardiovascular unit, so she immediately went there. She cringed when she first saw Tara. Her long hair was so matted that it looked "like a huge bird's nest." She had one earring on and was in shock. Tara was ecstatic to see her friend and wept uncontrollably. Tara pleaded for Sarah to find her family, and she promised that she would, bringing great comfort to Tara.

After searching desperately throughout the hospital, Sarah found Rylee and Nyla in the pediatric ward. The clothes they had worn during the tornado were replaced by hospital gowns, but their long blond hair was so matted that it looked like it had been cut short. They had been given snacks and were coloring amid the intermittent blackouts at the hospital. Because the nurses knew Sarah, she was

Dr. John Cox and Tara share a hug at the first year anniversary of the tornado.

allowed to take them to see Tara. Sarah wrapped them in hospital blankets and took them upstairs. When Rylee and Nyla reunited with Tara, they hugged their mom with tears of joy. The girls had only minor cuts and a few bruises due to being completely covered by the mattress and Tara and Danny's bodies. Sarah told Tara that she was going to take the little girls to her mom's house and care for them there. Rylee and Nyla behaved like little angels; (Vickie told Tara later) they did not cry or complain once. Vicki took them home and washed off the dirt, grime, and debris that were stuck like glue to their scalps. She had to change the water in the bathtub several times before it was clear of fragments. Although knowing that her girls were in Vickie's care, gave Tara solace, Vicki had unfortunately not been able to find Danny. She had been stationed at the morgue for over two hours and gratefully knew at least he was not there.

Chapter 5

Path of Destruction

According to the National Weather Service (NWS) in Springfield, Missouri, the tornado on May 22, 2011, had an eye that spanned the length of three football fields. Tornados with an eye are quite rare with the previous one occurring in Greensburg, Kansas in 2007. The tornado was the convergence of two storm systems: one in Northeast Oklahoma and the other in Southeast Kansas. The multi-vortex tornado had two or more small, strong sub-vortices that circled in the center of the larger tornado's circulation.

While Tara and Danny were recovering in the hospital, they were unaware of the destruction and devastation that the tornado had dealt to other parts of the city. The seventh deadliest storm in U.S. history was six miles long and with a one-mile wide swath, made its way slowly through parts of Joplin, killing 161 people and injuring more than a 1000.

Over 10,000 homes, buildings, (including twenty-eight churches), and apartments were either damaged or destroyed, and 18,000 cars were totaled. With wind speeds of 200 miles an hour, the tornado wiped out one-half of the schools in Joplin, including the high school which fortunately held its graduation at Missouri Southern State University that day. Because of the catastrophic state of the city, ambulances came from as far as 200 miles away. Joplin Memorial Hall and McAuley Catholic High School became triage centers, and temporary morgues were being set up all over the city.

St. John's Regional Medical Center was hit hard; windows were blown out, and there were massive gouges in various parts of the structure. The entire building was turned four inches on its axis. Because of the impending violent weather, a *Code Gray* was issued by the hospital twenty minutes before the tornado hit. A *Code Gray* is announced over the hospital's public address system indicating a need

Blown out windows were part of the damage of St. John's Medical Center.

for an emergency management response and can include severe weather, severe pollution, an act of terrorism, or a confrontational person who does not have a visible weapon. To obtain accreditation a *Code Gray* drill is practiced at least twelve times during the year. This single action resulted in saving many lives.

Organized chaos ensued at the hospital as the doctors and nurses were trying to evacuate and treat people at the same time. The hospital immediately lost power, the ceiling sprinklers continue to pour, and the smell of natural gas was prevalent. Doctors operated with flash lights, and due to loss of power, the medicine cabinets automatically locked. Hospital personnel had to use fire axes to open them while nurses used their hands to squeeze the resuscitator bags to keep patients alive. After ninety minutes, the hospital was completely evacuated. It was miraculous that only six fatalities occurred there that day.

Chapter 6

Healing and Recovery

Hours after the tornado hit, Eric and Katie Gilbert were trying to contact all their friends and family to make sure they were safe. Eric was the assistant pastor of Forest Park Baptist Church where the Graves were members. Tara and Danny had met the Gilberts in January 2011 at a meeting of a newly formed church organization called Life Group.

After Katie had located many of her family and friends on Monday, she called the Graves, but to no avail. Desperate for information about them, she then contacted Trisha Fisher, Tara's childhood friend. Trisha informed Katie that Tara was at Freeman Hospital, Rylee and Nyla were not injured, and Danny was at a hospital in Oklahoma. Katie immediately journeyed to the hospital to check on her friend. The trip took an hour and twenty minutes longer than normal due to all the roadblocks in town. To add to the grief of the previous day, there were more tornado warnings issued on Monday and Tuesday which caused much despair.

When Katie entered Tara's room, she did not recognize her friend. Tara still had grass and dirt in her hair but managed a smile. Tara was resting comfortably after the surgery the previous night but was still in pain. During their visit, Katie realized for the first time that the Graves' home had been destroyed. She did not hesitate in offering her home to the family. With grateful tears, Tara accepted the magnanimous offer and once again counted her blessings.

When Katie left the hospital, she picked up Rylee and Nyla, who had been staying with Danny's Grandma, and brought them to her home. The girls were excited about having playmates. The Gilberts lived twenty miles from Joplin with their three children: Dantley, seven; Bentley, five; and Skyley, eleven months. Their home was a 4000 square foot, four-bedroom house with a basement and was spacious enough to accommodate both families. The union of the two families would prove to be the best medicine for the healing of both the physical and emotional scars that the tornado had dealt.

Organized chaos was an understatement for the stress of the following days. Eric Gilbert, who was a victim of severe migraines, was losing weight and could not function daily. So he went to the hospital the Monday after the tornado. While Katie's sister-in-law, Lisa Lassiter, stayed with all five of the children, Katie met her husband at the hospital at the same time Trisha Fisher was bringing Tara to the Gilbert home. Tara stayed in the master bedroom on the first floor because she could not walk or climb stairs. The first few nights Tara was incoherent and highly medicated due to the severe pain. By the third night she could administer her own medications. Danny did not join the family then because he was not released from the hospital until later.

A few days after arriving at the Gilbert's home, Tara for the first time removed the bandages from her leg which was still extremely swollen and sore. She had a feeling that her leg was not healing properly, so Katie called a friend, Megan Ritchie, who was a Registered Nurse and asked her to stop by the house and check Tara's leg. After her observation Megan advised Tara to go immediately to the hospital. The pain was again excruciating as Tara walked on crutches to get to the car. Trisha drove her to the hospital amid screams of pain. Tara waited for hours in the ER and was finally admitted to the hospital. She stayed two days while the infection in her leg was addressed.

Since Rylee and Nyla had lost everything as well, Katie took them to TJ Maxx to shop. She bought them clothes, toys, swimming suits and most importantly, new pinkies (blankies). Katie decided they should name their pinkies, so the fun that ensued took their minds off their current predicament. It was a fun day for Rylee and Nyla to get out, just be little girls, and forget about the present.

Dantley and Bentley, although young, were also quite affected by the tornado. The boys took the girls under their wings and nurtured them. Bentley was Nyla's protector and made sure she was happy and safe at all times. The maturity of the young boys was truly commendable. A bond was developed instantly between the children, and the little girls were and are still considered part of the Gilbert family – a bond that is still strong today.

With five children in the house between the ages of seven years and eleven months, life was extremely chaotic for several weeks. The Gilberts tried to make daily life as normal as possible. When the Rylee and Nyla would get scared or tired, cartoons provided a great escape. The four older children always had great fun playing outside together during the early spring. Once the boys took old T-shirts and made them into football jerseys while the girls dressed as cheerleaders. Although the girls were resilient and adjusting to their new life, bedtime proved to be very hard for them. The quiet and darkness in the new house led to many tearful nights.

Rylee and Nyla Graves playing with Bentley and Dantley Gilbert days after the tornado.

Rylee, Nyla, Dantley, Bentley, and Skyley having fun in April 2014.

As the city of Joplin was recovering with the help of numerous volunteers and agencies all across the nation, the love and support for the Graves family was immeasurable. Everyone was available to help in any way possible. Eric's dad, Vern Gilbert, affectionately named Pa Pa, bought sacks and sacks of food and snacks for the children. They joked that he looked like Santa Claus coming through the door. There was such a copious amount of clothing donated to the family; the living room looked like a hoarder's house. Because there were so many items delivered, it took hours to separate the useable items from those not needed. Generosity continued pouring in. When the Gilberts left to attend a friend's wedding in Florida, meals were delivered every evening by church members, and the Life Group members even donated a car to the family. Blessings continued to abound just as the physical and emotional wounds began to heal.

Tara Graves and Katie Gilbert cooking at the Gilbert home in 2013.

During the weeks at the Gilbert home, Tara was slowly healing physically, but her disposition was declining as the reality of that fateful day became real. Weeks after the tornado, she asked Katie to take her shopping, so she could get out of the house. The two friends shopped and laughed; this was the first time Katie had seen Tara smile since the storm. There was finally a spark of joy. After they left the store, Tara asked to go by Connecticut Avenue. She had not been there since the day of the tornado. Despite massive roadblocks, they arrived at the pile of rubble that was once the family's home. By then it was dark, and Katie kept the headlights pointed towards the remains of the home that Tara had loved. It was "like Armageddon; the scene took our breath away." As far as they could see, there was no break in the wreckage. Katie said, "It looked like a bomb had gone off." No words were spoken for several minutes; then Tara looked down and saw a piece of her china. She picked it up, slowly brushed her finger across the surface, and kept repeating, "Here's my china!" Because the family dog Jack was still missing, she started screaming for him over and over and began sobbing uncontrollably. Comprehension of the unbelievable reality of the death and destruction finally dawned on her when she whispered, "It's a miracle."

The vast injuries that both Danny and Tara received healed progressively. Tara would be on a walker for four months and under the care of Dr. Donald Cotton at Freeman Wound Care for six months. Danny had a two-month recovery time. Both have numerous visible scars that are daily reminders of that day and the miracle.

Chapter 8

Finding a New Home

One of the most arduous tasks that the Graves faced after the tornado was finding a new place to call home. They had searched Joplin for a rental house for weeks, but all the houses had quickly been rented by the numerous storm victims before Tara and Danny were released from the hospital. After spending weeks with the Gilberts, the Graves knew they must find a home soon. Again, hope was on the horizon.

The long weeks of physical pain and emotional suffering were taking their toll on Tara, so she called her cousin, Lauren Webster, for comfort and support. Lauren asked her to come to Springfield, Missouri, and stay with her for a few days. During that visit Lauren and her sister, Elisha Nelson, thought Tara needed some fresh air, so they went for a drive around the city. Tara spotted a house for rent in the Phelps Grove neighborhood that she thought would be perfect for her family. She called the number on the sign and contacted Willie Grega.

Willie Grega, a high school choral director at Parkview High School in Springfield, managed the house near the Missouri State University campus for a friend. It was a bungalow style house with three bedrooms, two baths, and a basement. College students usually occupied the house, and many times left it in a ramshackle state. It had been vacant since the beginning of May, and still there were no renters by the first of June.

Willie told Tara the house was unlocked, so she could go inside. Tara opened the door and instantly fell in love with it. She knew then that it had to be the Graves' new home. Danny later called Willie and told him that his family was relocating from Joplin and needed a house with a basement. It never occurred to Willie that the Graves were tornado survivors.

Danny and Tara returned the next day to meet with Willie. When he saw them, he was shocked. Tara used a walker and had a cast on her right leg up to her knee. She walked at a snail's pace, and it was painful for her to climb the three steps to the porch or travel to the basement. Danny had a cast on his arm, scratches, and deep wounds on his face, head, and arms. Willie then saw the two precious girls who looked perfect with their bright spirit and smiling faces.

Willie thought the family looked like refugees and was hesitant to rent to them because the Graves had lost all their official documents. They had no social security cards, drivers' licenses, and no birth certificates - absolutely nothing. Willie took a leap of faith and rented to them unconditionally.

Tara and Danny asked Willie a few questions, looked at one another, and said this was the place for them. They filled out a renter's application, and Willie had to believe that all the information was true. His curiosity got the best of him, though, so he Googled their names later that day. He could not believe what he found and was moved to tears. Their names had been on the list of the missing tornado victims; their descriptions on the list verified their identity. That same day the entire family went to Hank's Fine Furniture and bought a table and chairs, two twin mattresses, and a king-size mattress to be delivered the very next day.

Danny, Tara, and the girls spent the night at Lauren's and started the process of building a new life on June 21, 2011, just a day shy of a month after the tornado. The family of four moved into their new home on Delmar St. in Springfield with only five plastic tubs full of their possessions. As they put the tubs on the floor in the empty house, an echo reverberated. They slowly looked at every inch that was vacant and knew starting over was not going to be easy. Again there were mournful tears about the past but also joyful tears for the opportunity and the gift of a future. They took a deep breath and thanked God for each other and all they had. They truly felt blessed. The transition in their new home was a daily challenge. The girls kept their beds next to their parents for several weeks because both the girls and their parents needed each other's physical comfort. It was a slow process, but the family finally started to heal emotionally.

The family took one day at a time in their new town and home. Although they were eternally thankful for what they had, it was extremely hard to leave their hometown of Joplin. Not only had they lost all their possessions, they left behind their lives: all their immediate family, friends, neighbors, and the girls' playmates and friends at school. They felt extremely isolated and alone. Their church and faithful members of the congregation who had been their rock during the ordeal were eighty miles away. It was a hard time for the family, and they shed many tears, but the family, like the damaged trees in the storm began slowly to revive.

Tara, Danny, Rylee and Nyla were very lucky to have moved to the house on Delmar St. The young family across the street was truly happy to finally see young children in the neighborhood. The Barks family - Bo, Rachel, Noah, and Ava - were the first to welcome them to the area. Willie had informed Bo and Rachel that the Graves were tornado victims.

Because of Tara's injuries, Bo and Rachel did not see her much the first few months, but Danny was always arriving each day with various items in his SUV that he had bought. Everything had been destroyed in the tornado, so the family had to replace every item that was normally found in a home. When they first moved in, they wanted to make a list of what they needed but had to laugh because they had no pen or paper on which to write it.

Bo helped Danny with unloading the daily trips to stores, and thus their friendship began. It was a slow process, but gradually the Graves began to share small bits of their ordeal. This helped the family achieve a kind of catharsis. The smallest comment would evolve into the most colorful story. Six weeks after the move, Noah, who was four, was playing with the girls in their backyard. That night Noah came home and started spinning in circles. Bo inquired what he was doing, and Noah said he was a tornado and that the girls were telling him how to spin like one.

Although the girls were thriving, they were dealing with the effects of the tornado in their own childlike way.

After a month on Delmar Street, the Graves invited the Barks family over for dinner. The adults had an enjoyable evening with great food, fun, and conversation while the four children played. To this day Bo still claims that Danny makes the best steaks in the world. Little by little the families started to bond, and there became a steady path between the houses. Tara and Rachel would visit while the children played outside; the Graves were finally getting acclimated to having a normal life again. With the help of Bo and Rachel, the Graves' circle of friends grew. The Barks would have play dates for the children and invite friends to their house, and gradually the Graves were meeting new people and feeling like part of a community. The Barks and the Gebkens - Richard, April, Conner, and Hudson - soon became the Graves' closest friends in Springfield. As time passed, the Graves' personal story of survival was revealed to their friends on many different occasions.

Rylee and Nyla Graves, Conner Gebken, Noah Barks, Olivia and Carsen Van Camp enjoy a swim in the lake.

Rylee Graves, Conner Gebken, and Debbie Fleitman strike a pose
during a party at the Graves' home.

Not wanting to let the girls out of their sight, Tara and
Danny were hesitant to enroll their girls in school the
following August. Rylee entered kindergarten at Sunshine
Elementary, but Danny and Tara wanted to keep Nyla at
home. However, the Barks and Gebkens both had their
children in Westminster Presbyterian Church Parents' Day
Out, so Tara and Danny decided to enroll Nyla and felt
comfortable leaving her. Their new friend, April Gebken,
worked part-time at the school, and Tara would see her
every day. Nyla thrived there and began building
friendships of her own. Finally, after five months of
trauma, pain, anxiety, and fear, the Graves family had
found peace and comfort in a town and neighborhood as
they continued building a new normal.

Chapter 7

Jack

In addition to the devastating destruction, massive loss of lives, and thousands of injured survivors, there was the daunting task of sheltering and caring for the animals that survived the tornado. The Humane Society under the direction of Karen Aquino partnered with the American Society for the Prevention of Cruelty to Animals (ASPCA) and came to the aid of over 600 pets that were found after the tornado. Three donated warehouses served as shelters for the animals: one building was for cats, one for dogs, and one for injured pets for which the society had been able to contact the owners. Over 100 volunteers from all over the nation arrived in Joplin to help render aid. The pets were given medical attention, food, vaccines, and a secure place to live. Along with their owners, the pets' lives had been turned upside down. Many residents whose houses had been destroyed were frantically looking for their pets; these valued companions were the only thing that many victims had left. Although many pets were reunited with their owners, a month later there were still hundreds of pets at the shelter.

The last time the Graves family had seen Jack was when they were getting in the car to go to the hospital; then he disappeared. The Graves began looking for Jack the second day they were in the hospital. They searched *Facebook*, *Craigslist*, and the Humane Society. Family and friends desperately searched for two months. Then Robyn Crosby, a friend of Danny's who worked at the Banfield Pet Hospital in Joplin and had taken care of Jack during his yearly vaccinations and examinations, saw a *Facebook* post from one of her friends. It was a picture of a dog that resembled Jack, and she was quite sure it was he. The Graves had been contacted with numerous pictures of dogs that people thought might be Jack, so when Tara got the call from Robyn, she was skeptical. Robyn sent the picture she believed to be Jack, and Tara received it when she and the little girls were in Hobby Lobby. They were so overwhelmed that they all started sobbing uncontrollably. Tara immediately called Willie, their landlord, questioned him about a pet deposit and asked if she could bring Jack home. Willie happened to be in Home Depot when he received the call and was again moved to tears. He told them, "Go get the dog!" The family was ecstatic to be reunited with their pet. Tara's *Facebook* post that day said it all: "Our dog Jack has been found!!! God is good!! God is good!! God is good!!"

A local family had found Jack the day of the tornado, and he had been only five blocks away from their Connecticut home all this time. They had not notified anyone because they selfishly wanted to keep Jack as their pet. Remarkably, he survived that day with only a few scratches. He still cries when it thunders, and fireworks make him go crazy. But like the Graves, he is a true survivor.

FOUND

ANOTHER COMPANION REUNITED WITH THEIR FAMILY

NAME:

Jack

GENDER:
Male

BREED:
GERMAN SHEPHERD

COLOR:
Black, Brown & Tan

WEIGHT:
70 lbs.

HEIGHT:
32 in.

ADDITIONAL INFO:
Jack was last seen at Connectict Avenue and 20th Street right after the tornado hit Joplin. He did not appear to have any injuries. His

TAG NUMBER:
10001123

 **Find My Animal**
FOR HOUSEHOLD PETS

WWW.FINDMYANIMAL.COM
1-888-703-FIND
(3463)

The Humane Society posted information about lost pets.

Chapter 9

A Second Chance

Only a few minutes changed the lives of the Graves family forever. Days after the tornado, the reality hit that they had nothing left. All their material possessions were swept away and vanished, but they all felt more blessed than they had a week before the tornado. They vowed never again "to take things for granted, nor to allow physical things that they had to define them." They were never angry about their fate and only cried when they realized all the help and support they had received from their friends, family, and people they never knew. They felt that they were given a second chance in life. The slate had been wiped clean, and all their petty grievances and complaints were no longer important. The tragedy made them realize that life is short and that the hand of God was on them that day. They truly believe that God and His angels were the reasons their lives had been spared. Danny knows that he survived that day for a purpose but continues to have much internal conflict with just what that purpose really is and why God chose to save him.

Many changes have occurred in the family since May 22, 2011. When there are impending storms, Danny and Tara get little sleep. There are many restless hours spent on the couch at night. Danny has four weather apps on his cell phone and connects with amateur storm watchers on *Facebook*. They still internally panic and have anxiety attacks even on sunny days when the tornado sirens are tested and will never live in a house that does not have a

Rylee and Nyla's helmets are always in the Graves' basement.

basement or a storm shelter. The basement of their house serves as a tornado shelter, and it is stocked with food and all the provisions the family would need in time of crisis. It is their second home during tornado season, and they have spent many nights there since their move to Springfield. The girls have their books, games, and their own brown and pink helmets for safety. During violent storms Tara sings "You Are My Sunshine" to calm her daughters. All their personal papers and documentation are stored there as well. They will never again risk having a complete lack of identity.

Seventeen months after the tornado, I observed Rylee and Nyla at my daughter's home as they watched the *Katy Perry Movie*. They were both full of vitality: fun-loving, talking, giggling, and enjoying life as any five and seven year old would. Children are the most resilient creatures on earth, but watching them that night, I could not imagine their experience, fear, and anxiety of springtime storms ahead. As time heals their emotional wounds, they will travel to adulthood with a greater appreciation of living each day to its fullest.

Developments

- A year after the tornado a woman from Pennsylvania, who came to Joplin to volunteer during the recovery efforts, found a sonogram about five miles from Joplin and mailed the picture to Ozark OB/GYN. One of the office staff looked up the file and confirmed it was Nyla Graves. Tara received a call from their office in Joplin, and the nurse asked if she was a storm victim and if she had given birth to a child in 2007. When Tara answered yes to both questions, she was told that the doctor's office had Nyla's sonogram. It was one of happiest days in Tara's life. She had lost everything that was a memory of the girls' births in the tornado, so this physical memento was a blessing.
- The Graves never found the man who drove them to the hospital.
- The Jacuzzi bathtub where the Tara and her daughters took their initial cover was never found, but the smoker in their yard was not touched by the tornado. The family still has it at their home in Springfield.

- Eight months after the tornado, St. John's Regional Medical Center was torn down, and the new St. John's (now Mercy) is being built two miles away.

Three Years Later

After over three years of healing and rebuilding, both Danny and Tara have gone back to work. Tara is employed by Chico's in Springfield, and Danny and his cousin started an internet business called Dot-Social Marketing Group. Danny also is employed as an AT&T sales supervisor at

One year later Danny, Tara, Rylee, and Nyla standing at the spot where they survived.

Sunrise Communication. Rylee is in the second grade, and Nyla started kindergarten this year, with both attending Sunshine Elementary School. Jack is still the girls' constant companion and is thriving. Life could never be better on Delmar St. in Springfield, Missouri.

Afterward

Living in Texas all my life, I have constantly experienced the threats of tornados. Texas springtime is synonymous with tornados. Texans know the signs, heed the warnings, and prepare for the worst. When I was a young child, my family and I spent many nights in our backyard green circular cellar. My dad was from Pennsylvania and was deathly afraid of storms, so there was much time spent there. Five children and two adults made for a cozy, claustrophobic experience. As an adult I have also spent many hours in the downstairs bathroom with my daughters, crowded with pillows, stuffed animals, and blankets when the tornado sirens blared. My family and I have been lucky with just a few damaged shingles, broken tree limbs, and toppled trees. We Texans have a healthy respect for the wrath of pounding rain, hail, and wind that accompanies a tornado.

This being said, after many hours of researching and writing this book, my mind still cannot encompass the magnitude and power of nature at its worst. The pictures of the Joplin tornado's obliteration paint a collage of turmoil and incomprehensible destruction, but words cannot do justice to the aftermath that is left for all who survived.

My daughter and I visited a snow-covered Joplin in February 2014 on one of the coldest days of the year. Although it had been well over two years since the tornado, the city still bore the scars of that fateful day. The massive empty lot where a hospital once stood, the new neighborhoods of rebuilt houses dotted with the old ones that somehow were spared that day, and the building of the new high school were reminders of the demon that touched the earth that Sunday in May. I journeyed through the same doors of Freeman Hospital where thousands of victims were taken on May 22, 2011. I saw the huge waiting room that was once crammed with the injured and dying, and I could only imagine the chaos. The most shocking sight that day was the stark realization that along the path of the tornado, there were no trees - None! As Patrick Tuttle, the director of the Joplin Convention and Tourist Bureau, stopped his truck at the top of a hill, we looked left to see a vital city with neighborhoods, houses, and trees, and to the right, we could see the horizon. The scene was like two separate cities that had been pasted together at an intersection. The absence of trees told the story of the fury of the tornado and how it twisted and turned as it zigzagged through the city.

As I walked through the lot where the Graves' house once stood, emotion overtook me. To know that once a beautiful family called this piece of earth home and to comprehend all that was gone in minutes was heart wrenching. I viewed the place where the three trees that helped save their lives had been located on their lot, but only stumps remained. The slab of their home was a concrete reminder of what once existed.

The lot where the Graves' home once stood is still vacant – 2014.

The Miracle of the Human Spirit monument is located in
Cunningham Park.

Joplin immediately began to rebuild days after the tornado and continues to take pride in the recovery and the effort to bring their city to the place it was before or even better. The one year anniversary was a celebration of life and continued growth and revitalization of their city. A plaque with the 161 fatalities was unveiled in Cunningham Park as well as the silver wristband monument named the Miracle of the Human Spirit. It stands and remains the mantra for past, present, and future of Joplin, Missouri.

The plaque honoring the 161 victims of the tornado is located in Cunningham Park.

Acknowledgments

As in any endeavor in life, it takes a plethora of people and resources to complete a task at hand. So many people and websites helped me through this process with either information or support through many different means.

The abundant information online about the tornado and the city of Joplin helped immensely while writing this book. I consulted www.city-data.com, www.stltoday.com, and www.joplinmo.org and located statistics and demographics about the city of Joplin. *Joplin 5:41 When a Monster Storm Shattered a Missouri Town but Didn't Break Its Spirit* by the *Kansas City Star* staff gave a comprehensive overview of the damage of the area as well as fatalities and injuries that day. Several sites were instrumental in providing scientific data and information about the anatomy of an EF-5 tornado and climate conditions in the Ozark area. The information from www.livescience.com and www.ncdc.noaa explained the eye of the tornado and the statistics about Tornado Alley. Facts about May 22, 2011, and the aftermath were made available from www.news-leader.com and www.helpjoplin.com. Also the site www.kansascity.com provided detailed information about the damage and rescue effort at St. John's Medical Center.

Kudos and accolades go to Katie Gilbert, Willie Grega, Bo Barks, and Sarah Cox Horton for invaluable information about May 22, 2011, and the days and weeks to follow.

Much gratitude goes to Patrick Tuttle for the tour of Joplin, and the personal narrative about the city. His knowledge and contributions were essential components to complete this book. His also generously granted me the use of several of his personal photos. The graciousness of Donna Miller is also greatly appreciated.

This book would not be complete without the editing of my dear friend and teacher Patty Bowden. She has been my mentor and "go to person" for many years. Also, thanks to my friend Deloris Glenn for her discerning eye while editing this book and her helpful input in so many areas. Their feedback was priceless.

I also have family and friends who were my ardent cheerleaders throughout this process and were always there for encouragement and support: my little sis Mary Klement who has always been there through thick and thin; sister-in-law Lenora Isenhour who is truly a loving sister to me, and Granny and Grandpa for being the best grandparents in the world.

Jane Dobson and Joanie Pulte, you will always be by my side through tears and laughter.

Thanks to my parents for sacrificing so much to allow me to attend college and become a teacher.

Much love goes to my family who are the lifeline to my existence. Nothing could be possible without their love and support.

Richard, I could not have finished this book without your technical expertise. Thanks for your patience and the many hours you gave to transform these words into a book. I could not have done this without you. Thanks **James**, for your support and the laptop that allowed me to have a change of venue when I wrote.

Conner, **Hudson**, and **Nora**, you are the sunshine in my life. The joy you bring me is the essence of my soul. I love you so much!

April and **Katie**, my life would not be complete without you. You have always been my most devoted supporters encouraging me always to continue my quest. Thanks for all your months of help with so many details and your daily encouragement.   Thanks April for the wonderful photographs of the Joplin area and the Graves family. Your photos grace this book and meticulously capture that moment in time.   Katie, thanks for being brutally honest after you read the first draft and for designing the cover that depicts the devastation of that day.   **Allen,** thanks for taking a ride with me on another project. You are my rock, and your love is immeasurable.

Most of all thank you to Tara, Danny, Rylee, and Nyla. Writing this book has been an incomprehensible journey. You have become a daily part of my life for over two years and have allowed me to script your darkest moments and the agony of your souls. Your beautiful young daughters will become strong, independent women and will benefit immensely from the love and guidance you have given them. Your family will always be with me.

Danny, Nyla, Rylee, and Tara Graves

33271428R00044

Made in the USA
Charleston, SC
10 September 2014